Contents

Introduction

The exact origins of chess are clouded in time. It is reported to have started somewhere between the Middle East and the Far East about 3000 years ago. The game arrived in Europe as merchant traders returned home from their travels in the time of Marco Polo.

Except for a slight modification to the laws of chess about 200 years ago, the basic game has remained unchanged. These days discussions and amendments revolve around competitive rules. The most important of these contentious points is the *If you touch your piece you must move it!* rule. It is always best to play to this rule, even when the game is a short one played only for fun in a few spare minutes.

Chess is great fun. Once you have learnt the basic rules from this book and have played your friends at home, work or school, look for a wider variety of opposition, someone who might play a different order of moves to yourself.

It is estimated that over half of the households in the Western world own a chess set. Your national governing body will have lists of local chess clubs and suppliers of equipment and books, plus details of competitions.

Enjoy your chess!

Acknowledgements
Text by Adam Raoof and Tony Corfe of Tournament Chess Supplies.
Photography by Mike Ellis.
Illustrations by Adam Raoof, produced using NicBase and NicPrint software.

Note Throughout the text players are referred to individually as 'he'. This should, of course, be taken to mean 'he or she' where appropriate.

Basics

The chess board

The game of chess is played on a square board with 64 squares coloured alternately light and dark. This is the battlefield on which the two armies meet.

Setting up

The board is always placed so that there is a white square to the *right* of each player.

In this book, as is the convention in most chess books, white plays *up* the board and black plays *down* the board. Each player has 16 men, consisting of eight pieces and eight pawns.

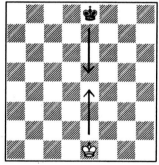

Fig. 1

Ranks and files

Each line of squares running across the board is called a *rank*, and is referred to from white or black's point of view. There are therefore eight ranks.

Each column of squares running up the board is referred to as a *file*. There are eight files.

The centre

The area which lies in the no-man's-land between the two armies is known as the *centre* of the board and is usually the scene of the heaviest fighting between the white and black armies.

Pieces placed either in or near the centre are said to be *centralised* and gain greater scope.

Diagonals

Diagonals run across the board along squares of the same colour. There are white squared diagonals and dark squared diagonals.

Whereas ranks and files are of equal length – eight squares – the diagonals are of varying lengths and are often referred to as *long* or *short* diagonals.

Pieces and pawns

Each side has eight *pieces* and eight *pawns*, arranged symmetrically on opposite sides of the chess board. The two armies are different colours, normally black and white, to distinguish them from each other.

There are five different pieces, to which we can give relative values.

3

The King

(Value – immeasurable.)

When an enemy piece threatens the King with capture, the King is said to be *in check*.

The aim of chess is to *checkmate* the opposing King by placing him in a situation where he cannot avoid capture.

The King is therefore a priceless piece – when the King is lost, the game ends immediately!

The King starts off in the centre of the first rank but spends most of the early part of the game tucked safely away in the corner of the board where the enemy forces would find it difficult to attack.

The King can move in *any* direction along ranks, files and diagonals, but only one square at a time, and *never* to or through a square which is attacked by enemy men.

In fig. 2 white's King can move to any of the marked squares.

The Queen

(Relative value – 9 points.)

The Queen is your most powerful and valuable piece. Therefore she emerges only after the protection from less valuable pieces has been assured!

The Queen, like the King, can move in *any* direction along ranks, files and diagonals but also along *any number* of unoccupied squares. This makes the Queen exceptionally good for rounding up stray enemy pieces.

In fig. 3, white's Queen can move to any of the marked squares.

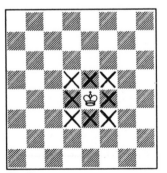

Fig. 2

▲ *King (left) and Queen*

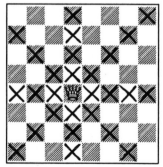

Fig. 3

The Rooks

(Relative value – 5 points each.)

The two Rooks can move any number of squares, but only in a straight line along open files and across open ranks. Open files only become available to Rooks once some pawns have been exchanged; therefore Rooks are not normally brought into action until later in the game.

The Queens and Rooks are normally referred to as the *major pieces*.

In fig. 4 white's Rook can move to any of the marked squares.

The Bishops

(Relative value – 3 points each.)

Each side begins the game with a Bishop on a white square and a Bishop on a black square, referred to as *light* and *dark squared Bishops* respectively. The two Bishops begin the game on the right of the King and on the left of the Queen, and are known as the *King's Bishop* and *Queen's Bishop* respectively.

The two Bishops can move any number of squares along diagonals of white squares if the piece started the game on a white square, and black squares if on a black square. This means that a Bishop can pass freely *between* lines of both friendly and enemy men. They can never move to attack or cross squares of the opposite colour.

The Bishops are ideal long range pieces to employ in a lightning tactical strike on the enemy King.

In fig. 5, white's Bishop can move to any of the marked squares.

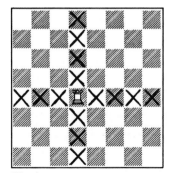

Fig. 4

▲ *Rook* (left) *and Bishop*

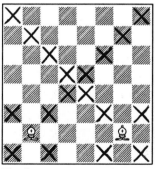

Fig. 5

The Knights

(Relative value – 3 points each.)

The Knight moves in a rather peculiar way, a short hop which resembles an L-shape. The Knight can also do something that no other piece can do: like any decent cavalryman, it can leap *over* both friendly and enemy men.

Due to this fact, the Knights are often the first pieces to be developed and are better placed in the *centre* of the board rather than at the edge, since from the centre of the board a Knight can reach many more squares on its next move. From the edge of the board the Knight can reach four squares; in the centre it can reach eight. If by some unfortunate chance a Knight ends up in the corner of the board, it is reduced to just two possible squares. (*See* fig. 6.)

The Knights and Bishops are usually referred to as the *minor* pieces and are nominally of the same value, though in practice the position will sometimes favour Knights (generally 'closed' positions where there are chains of pawns locked together which might obstruct movement) or Bishops ('open' positions with few pawns where the Bishops can command long diagonals).

The pawns

(Relative value – 1 point each.)

The pawns are the footsoldiers in a game of chess, the vanguard of the army. Each pawn can choose to move one square, or two on its first move only, and can only move forwards. (*See* fig. 7.)

Pawns are unlike pieces in that while pieces capture in the same way that they move, pawns capture diagonally forwards, one square to the left or right. This means that great care must be taken when moving pawns, since every pawn move commits a

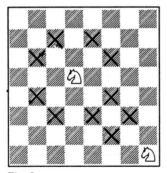

Fig. 6

▲ *Knight* (left) *and pawn*

Fig. 7

6

pawn to a square on a semi-permanent basis. In the middlegame this can give rise to certain distinctive positional features which we will identify.

Promotion

Humble pawns are not expected to survive the battle. Consequently pawns which survive the long journey into the heart of the enemy encampment are destined for great things!

When a pawn reaches the eighth rank it is *promoted*, in recognition of its great achievement, to any piece except another King! In practice, this usually means promoting to a Queen.

Notation

It is very important to have some means of scoring or recording your games in order to be able to play through them later where, away from the heat of the battle, you can analyse the game, perhaps to see when you could have improved your play.

The system of shorthand in common use in the UK is called *algebraic* notation. In this book we will be using international *figurine* algebraic, where each piece is represented by a figurine symbol. The full board looks like this:

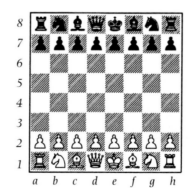

Fig. 8 ▶

Each square is given a unique co-ordinate, consisting of a letter and a number. The ranks are numbered from 1 to 8, from top to bottom, and always from white's point of view. The files are lettered from a–h, left to right, again from white's point of view. The pieces are referred to by either a figurine symbol or by a letter as follows:

King	♔	K	Queen	♕	Q
Rook	♖	R	Bishop	♗	B
Knight	♘	N (to avoid confusion with K for King)			

To describe the movement of a man you must specify the move number, the piece (pawns need not be identified) and the square it moves to, i.e. 1.♘f3 ♘f6 indicates that both sides have used their first move to bring their Knights out. Captures are shown by a cross – × – (♗×f6) and checks by a plus sign after the move (♕h5+). Checkmate is # or simply *mate*.

Additionally, writers will often use other symbols in annotating games: !(good move); ?(questionable move); !!(brilliant move); ??(blunder); 1–0 (black resigns); 0–1(white resigns); ½–½(draw).

A completed scoresheet

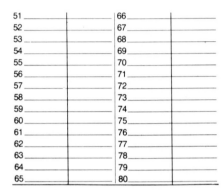

	White	Black		
1	e4	d5	26	
2	exd5	Qxd5	27	
3	Nc3	Qa5	28	
4	d4	Nf6	29	
5	Nf3	c6	30	
6	Bd2	Bg4	31	
7	h3	Bh5	32	
8	g4	Bg6	33	
9	Bc4	Qb6	34	
10	Qe2	e6	35	
11	0-0-0	Nbd7	36	
12	h4	h5	37	
13	g5	Ng8	38	
14	d5	cxd5	39	
15	Nxd5	Qd8	40	
16	Ne5	Bxc2	41	
17	Kxc2	Nxe5	42	
18	Qxe5	Rc8	43	
19	Bc3	Rxc4	44	
20	Nf6+	gxf6	45	
21	Rxd8+	Kxd8	46	
22	Qb8+	Kd7	47	
23	Rd1+	Kc6	48	
24	Qc8+		49	
25	1 — 0		50	

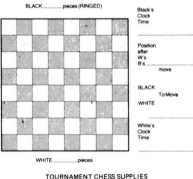

Capturing pieces

Capture pieces by occupying the square on which an enemy piece sits with your own piece. In fig. 9, each of white's pieces can capture black's pawn on e5.

Each side should aim to *capture* as many of the enemy pieces as possible. This reduces the ability of the other player to defend his King.

Exchanging pieces, on the other hand, simply reduces the number of pieces on each side like for like.

Fig. 9

Special moves

En passant

(Algebraic notation: *e.p.*)

When the game of chess was in its infancy, pawns could only move one square on their first move. This meant that pawns could seldom avoid capture by other pawns, since they would have to pass each other as they crossed the board.

The invention of the double-pawn move allowed pawns to evade capture and often led to rather slow, stodgy and cramped positions.

The modern form of the game was enlivened by the introduction of the *en passant* rule. If you choose to move a pawn two squares on its first move, it may then be captured by an enemy pawn on an adjacent file *en passant* (literally in French, *in passing*) as if it had only moved one square, but only if the capture was made immediately.

Fig. 10

In fig. 10, white can play 1.b4, and black has the option to capture the b pawn *en passant* by 1...c×b3 e.p. as if white had played 1.b3 (fig. 11).

To capture a pawn *en passant* is not compulsory (even though it may impress someone who doesn't know the rules). In any position you should only capture pawns if you think it is the best move.

In figs 12 and 13, if white plays 1.b4 black does not have the option to capture by 1...c×b3 since white's pawn moved just one square.

Fig. 11

Fig. 12

9

Fig. 13

Castling

(Algebraic notation: 0–0 or 0–0–0.)

This is the only time in the game when you are allowed to make two moves at once, and it is nearly always a good move!

Castling involves first moving the King two squares to the side, then jumping the Rook on that side over the King. A player may castle once during a game, on the queenside or on the kingside, subject to a few rules.

• Neither the King nor the Rook may have moved previously.

• The King must not move on to or pass over a threatened square.

• The King cannot castle while in check.

• Neither the King nor the Rook may pass over an occupied square.

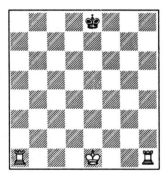

Fig. 14

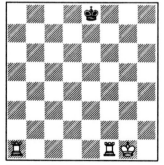

Fig. 15 – kingside castling

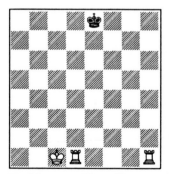

Fig. 16 – queenside castling

Starting and ending a game

It is a convention in chess that white always makes the first move. This gives the player with the white pieces a slight, but only a slight, advantage. Each player then takes his turn to make a move and *develop* his pieces to good squares.

A game is ended when one of the players delivers checkmate, although in practice most games are ended by *resignation* – a player may resign the game at any point if he is about to be mated or if he is in such a hopeless position that mate is inevitable.

The game may also end in a *draw* through:

• *lack of force* – neither side has enough material left to force checkmate
• *an agreed draw* – when the players 'share the point' by agreeing a draw
• *stalemate* – if the player to move has no legal move and is not in check, he is

said to be *stalemated*. In fig. 17 white, to move, played 1.♔g5? and realised that he had left black with no move – stalemate

Fig. 17

• *inability* to deliver mate with the material available in a specified number of moves
• *perpetual check* – a player who has committed his pieces to an attack but finds that he cannot deliver mate, can draw if he can demonstrate that his opponent cannot escape his checks. This is called *perpetual check*. Normally he only has to repeat the position three times to claim a draw.

Study fig. 18. White has *sacrificed the exchange* (given up a Rook for a minor piece) for an attack on black's King, and here white threatens 1.♕×h7 mate.

Black saw nothing wrong with winning more material but after 1...g×f6? 2.♕×f6+ ♔g8 3.♕g5+ he realised that white had a perpetual check and the game was drawn.

In fact, the more modest 1...♗f5 would have secured black's position and given him good winning chances.

Kessler – Cornell *(USA, 1976)*

Fig. 18

11

Common traps to avoid

A wise commander directs his attack at the enemy's weakest point. In chess this equates to squares left undefended or defended solely by the King, whose value makes it a poor defending piece.

In the opening position the weakest points are the squares f2 for white and f7 for black.

The following game shows how white can exploit this weakness to score a quick victory with a direct assault which claims countless beginners, until they learn better. Hence the name .....

Scholar's mate

1.e4   e5

Both sides secure a pawn in the centre.

Note that while neither pawn move is *in itself* a developing move, it permits each side, on its next move, to develop its King's Bishop.

2.♗c4

This develops the Bishop to an active square and eyes the f7 square.

2...   ♞c6
3.♕h5

White adds the power of his Queen to the attack, with a deadly threat.

3...   ♞f6??

Black could have defended by 3...g6.

4.♕×f7 mate

Fig. 19

Another spectacular and even quicker way to lose is .....

Fool's mate

1.f3?

A move which does nothing whatsoever to develop white's pieces and which weakens the sensitive short diagonal e1-h4 leading directly to white's King.

1...   e5
2.g4??   ♕h4 mate

White has been checkmated.

Fig. 20

Checks

In the normal course of a game it is not fatal to receive a check. You can defend against most checks by:

• capturing the piece which gives check
• interposing a piece, or as a last resort
• moving the King out of check.

For example, in the following opening white checks the black King as early as move three:

1.e4   c5
2.♘f3   d6
3.♗b5+

Fig. 21

Black cannot capture the enemy Bishop or move his King out of check – but he *may* block the check by interposing a piece by 3...♘c6, 3...♘d7 or 3...♗d7.

The only other legal move, 3...♛d7??, would be a terrible mistake. It would save the King but, after 4.♗×d7+ ♗×d7, lose the Queen (9 points) for just a Bishop (3 points).

There are, however, two lethal varieties of check.

Discovered check

When the action of a piece is unmasked by moving a piece from in front of it, it is called a *discovered attack*. When the subject of the attack is the enemy King, it is called a *discovered check*.

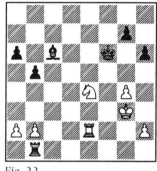

Fig. 22

In the above example black, in check, mistakenly played 1...♚e5? when white had the crafty discovered check 1.♘d2+, which wins the Rook on b1. The Rook on e2 gives discovered check.

13

Double check

It is sometimes possible to give check with two pieces simultaneously, a *double check*. In that event it is not possible to evade check by either of the first two methods outlined previously.

In fig. 23 white could play either 1.♖g4++ or 1.♖d7++, checking the black King on g7 with the Rook, and the Bishop on b2.

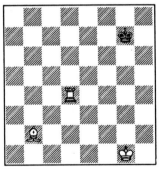

Fig. 23

In the following game black is mated using a discovered, double check!

Reti–Tartakower (*Vienna, 1910*)

1.e4	c6
2.d4	d5
3.♘c3	d×e4
4.♘×e4	♘f6
5.♕d3	e5?

This move does not lose a pawn. But it does lose *time*. In chess the unit of time is the *tempo* (plural tempi).

In fact, black spends so many *tempi* (so much time) in regaining it that he falls dangerously behind in development.

6.d×e5	♕a5+
7.♗d2	♕×e5
8.0–0–0	♘×e4?

Black appears to have won a pawn, but a nasty surprise awaits . . .

Fig. 24

9.♕d8+!!	♔×d8

Black has no choice but to capture the offered Queen.

10.♗g5++	♔c7
11.♗d8 mate!	

Tactics

Capturing pieces

Capturing enemy pieces is the most direct way to overwhelm the enemy! Deplete the enemy's forces and you reduce their ability to defend against attack.

Pieces are captured by occupying the square on which they stand and removing the captured pieces from the board.

The basic principle of chess tactics is that when a stronger piece is attacked by a weaker piece, it must give way, e.g. if a Queen is attacked by any of the enemy's pieces, or if a Rook is attacked by a Bishop or Knight. A pawn can, because of its low value, brush aside all the pieces.

En prise

When a piece is under attack, so that it may be captured on the next move, it is said to be *en prise*. Assuming that your opponent is not going to be so helpful as to leave his valuable pieces *en prise*, you will have to know some ways to trap them.

Combinations

When you put together a series of moves or tactical ideas to win a piece or give mate or even to destroy your opponent's pawn formation, this is called a *combination*.

Here are some of the standard tactical operations. Try to remember the crucial elements of the combinations rather than the exact positions since the ideas recur time and time again in varying forms.

Double attack

If you can manage to attack two or more pieces at once, then your opponent will have time only to remove one of them from danger before it is once more your turn to move. This many-pronged attack is often known as a *fork*.

For instance, in fig. 25 white can play 1.♘f7, a Knight fork which attacks both of black's Rooks. Black to move, saves one Rook by 1...♖de8,

but now white captures the other Rook with 2.♘xh8! This win of a Rook for a minor piece is known as *winning the exchange*.

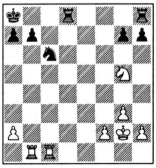

Fig. 25

In fig. 26, however, white does not appear to threaten anything, but with his next move he plays 1.♖d5!, forking both of the black Knights, winning at least one of them.

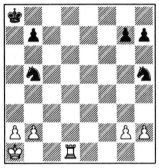

Fig. 26

The following example shows a more complex double attack.

Korchnoi – Portisch *(1968)*

White's last move had been the innocent 1.♘d5? Black, to move, played 1...♗×d5! 2.e×d5 g3!, attacking the Knight on c4 laterally with his Queen and threatening

Fig. 27

3...g×f2+, forking white's King and Rook. White had to lose material and, eventually, the game.

Veresov – Buslaev *(1963)*

Again, white conjured up the win of a piece from nothing with 1.♗×f6! ♗×f6. Normally, exchanging a Bishop for a Knight in such a fluid position would be a mistake. But black now had *two* unprotected pieces and after 2.♘d5! (discovering an attack on the black Queen and directly threatening the ♗f6) 2...♕×d2 3.♘×f6+ ♔h8 (if black plays 3...♔g7 to attack the

Knight, then 4.♘×e8+ wins more material) 4.♖×d2, white had won a piece by means of a double attack.

Fig. 28

Note that if white had castled on the queenside and had his King on c1, the combination would have failed because 2...♕×d2 would be check, giving black time to defend or remove his Bishop.

Skewers

Any number of pieces placed on the same rank, file or diagonal can fall foul of the *skewer*.

In fig. 29 black is threatening to take the white Queen with his Bishop, so white wisely moves his Queen from danger. But black then wins the exchange with 1...♗×a1. What happened?

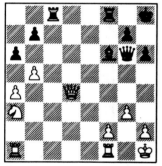

Fig. 29

White's pieces are *skewered* by the x-ray action of black's Bishop, which cuts through the Queen and when the Queen moves, through the Rook.

Fig. 30

Here, black to move plays 1...♖e8+ and white, being unable to deal with the attack on his King in any other way, is compelled to move his King 2.♔f4, allowing black to play 2...♖×e1.

Fig. 31

In this position, however, the location of the King and Queen has been reversed. If black now plays 1...♖(either)e8, attacking the Queen, white cannot move his Queen away as the King would then be under attack. This is known as a *pin*.

Pin

A *pin* occurs when a piece is *unable* to move because to do so would allow a more valuable piece to be captured. The Knight cannot pin another piece.

In fig. 32, black's Knight on e6 is pinned by the white Bishop and is unable to move. You can *never* move your King into check.

Fig. 32

Overloading

When a piece is defending more than one piece, it can become *overloaded*.

In fig. 33, the black Knight is not just defending white's threatened mate at g7, but also the Rook on d8. Therefore 1.♖×d8+ wins, since 1...♘×d8 allows 2.♕g7 mate!

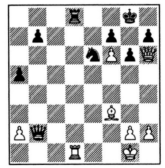

Fig. 33

Decoy

A commander uses a decoy to lure a sentry away from his post and on to dangerous ground. In chess you can use the same idea to tempt your opponent's defending pieces away from crucial squares.

In fig. 34, white's Rook is the only thing preventing black from promoting his g-pawn. Black wins by playing 1...♖d4+!, forking the white King and Rook. After 2.♖×d4 g1=♕ white could resign.

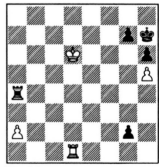

Fig. 34

In fig. 35, white took advantage of the position of his opponent's pieces by 1.♗×f7 ♖×f7 2.♕h8+!!, decoying the King on to a vulnerable square, where it falls prey to a devastating Knight fork, 2...♚×h8 3.♘×f7+ followed by 4.♘×g5 with the decisive material advantage of an extra Knight.

Petrosian – Spassky
(World Championship, 1966)

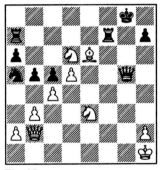

Fig. 35

In fig. 36, white won by 1.♖d7+!, which gave black two very unpleasant alternatives. Either 1...♚×d7 2.♘×f6+! ♖×f6 3.♕×e2 wins the Queen or 1...♚e6 2.♕d5 is mate.

Prins – Fuderer
(Rogaska Slatina, 1948)

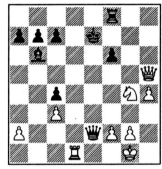

Fig. 36

In fig. 37, white found an unusual combination. First he played 1.♗c7!, skewering black's awkwardly placed Rook against his Queen. Black, of course, played 1...♖×c7. Then came 2.♕e5!, with the point that both 3.♕×c7 (winning the exchange) and 3.♕×g7 mate are threatened.

Spassky – Aronin *(USSR, 1973)*

Fig. 37

19

In fig. 38, once again black's undefended ♕a5 is the victim. White, by 1.♗f7+!, lured the black King out of safety. Black resigned himself to the loss of a piece after 1...♔f8 2.♗xg6 (the h-pawn is pinned) since the alternative 1...♔xf7 2.e6+ ♗xe6 3.♕xa5 wins on the spot.

Katalimov – Ilivitsky *(USSR, 1959)*

Fig. 38

Destroying the defender

In fig. 39, black's Knight is only defended by the Bishop on f6. White plays 1.♘xf6+ ♘xf6 2.♕xd4, winning a piece.

Fig. 39

Black's position looks solid enough in fig. 40, since his excellent Bishop on d4 secures both pawns in the centre and keeps white's pieces out.

But with 1.♖xd4!, white broke through and black resigned because after 1...exd4 2.♖e5+ ♔xg4 3.h3 or 3.f3 he is mated.

Petrosian – Ivkov *(1979)*

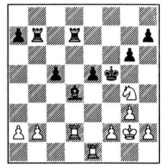

Fig. 40

Mating the King

The basic mating positions

The basic mating positions are fairly simple to master and apply. In all situations where you are playing against a bare King, the player trying to give mate has to first drive the enemy King to the edge of the board with his piece or pieces, usually assisted by his King.

The main trap to avoid is accidentally delivering stalemate! 1.♕e6 ♚b4 2.♕b6+ ♚c4 3.♕c6+ ♚b4 4.♔d3 ♚a5 5.♕b7 ♚a4 6.♔c4 ♚a5 7.♕b5 mate.

♔ & ♕ vs ♚

Fig. 41

Fig. 42

♔ & ♖ vs ♚

Fig. 43

This follows the same two principles but, because it involves a little finesse, takes a few more moves.
1.♔d3 ♚f4 2.♖f2+ ♚e5 3.♖f3! ♚d5 4.♖f5+ ♚c6 5.♔d4 ♚b6 (or 5...♚d6 6.♖f6+ driving the King back) 6.♖c5 ♚b7 7.♔d5 ♚b6 8.♔d6 ♚b7 9.♖b5+ ♚c8 (9...♚a6 10.♚c6 ♚a7 11.♖a5+ ♚b8 12.♖a4! ♚c8 13.♖a8 mate is a similar finish)10.♖b4! (or 10.♖b3 or 10.♖b2 or 10.♖b1, etc.) 10...♚d8 11.♖b8 mate.

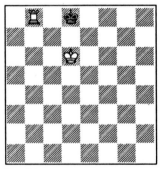

Fig. 44

This finesse, which involves playing a waiting move rather than continually checking to force black's King into a mating net, is called putting black in *zugzwang* (from the German for *compulsion to move*).

♔ & 2 ♗ vs ♚

Fig. 45

The process involves using the power of the two united Bishops to drive the King to a corner of the board where mate can be given. It is not possible to checkmate with only one Bishop against a bare King.

1.♗e3 ♚e5 2.♗e4 ♚d6 3.♔d4 ♚e6 4.♗f4 ♚d7 5.♔d5 ♚e7 6.♗e5 ♚f7 7.♗f5 ♚g8 8.♚e6 ♚f8 9.♗g6! ♚g8 10.♚f6
(not 10.♚e7?? stalemate) 10...♚f8 (or 10...♚h8 11.♚f7 mate) 11.♗d6+ ♚g8 12.♚g5 ♚g7 13.♗e4! ♚h8 14.♚h6 ♚g8 15.♗d5+ ♚h8 16.♗e5 mate.

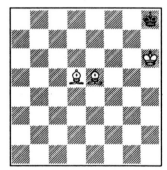

Fig. 46

The hardest way to give mate is with *Knight and Bishop*. White has to drive the King to the edge of the board and then to the corner which is the same colour as the Bishop.

Fig. 47

Checkmate in the middlegame

When you are playing a competitive game, your main aim will be to mate your opponent as directly as possible. You will need to look at and learn the following *mating patterns*, since they occur time and again in games played at every level.

Checkmating motifs

Back rank mate
This occurs when all the pieces have been developed and have left the back rank.

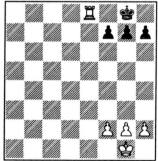

Fig. 48

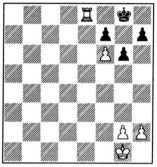

Fig. 49

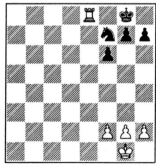

Fig. 50

Fig. 51

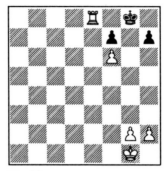

Fig. 52

Fig. 54

Fig. 53

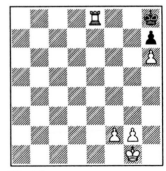

Fig. 55

♕ & ♗ battery

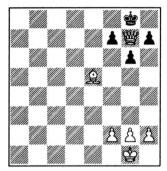

Fig. 56

Fig. 57

♕ & ♘

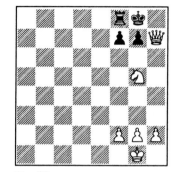

Fig. 58

♕ & ♙

Fig. 59

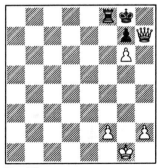

Fig. 60

♘ & ♗

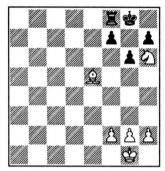

Fig. 61

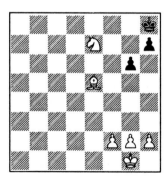

Fig. 62

2 ♗s

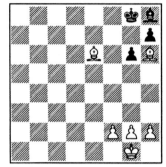

Fig. 63

2 ♖s

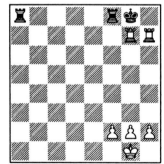

Fig. 64

♖ & ♘ mate

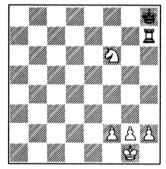

Fig. 65

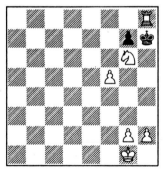

Fig. 66

26

Epaulette mate

So-called because the two Rooks flanking the King resemble the epaulettes on a uniform.

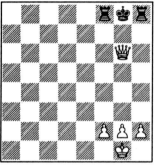

Fig. 67

Smothered mate

A famous case of smothered mate, one which is essential to learn, is *Philidor's Legacy*. (*See* figs 70 and 71.)

1.♘f7+ ♔g8 2.♘h6++! ♔g8
3.♕g8+!! ♖×g8 4.♘f7 mate.

Corridor mate

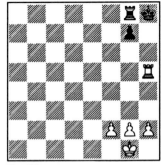

Fig. 68

Fig. 69

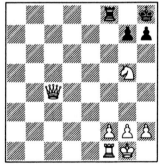

Fig. 70

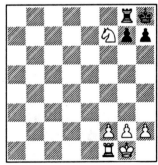

Fig. 71

The three phases of the game

Most games of chess share three features: an *opening*, a *middlegame* and an *endgame*.

Chess players know a great deal about their favourite opening variations and some of the resulting types of middlegame, but very few will know anything but the very basic elements of endgame theory.

The opening

In the opening phase of the game, both players attempt to develop their pieces in readiness to attack – and, of course, to interfere with the development of the opponent's forces.

We have already remarked that white gains a slight advantage by moving first, but this is usually not enough to gain a winning position.

Theoretically, since each player gets a turn to move, the game should always be roughly equal. However, the more *tempi* that you can gain to mobilise your pieces – by development, by checking your opponent's King and perhaps causing him to lose the right to castle, by sacrificing material or by preventing him from developing normally – the better prepared *you* will be in the middlegame.

One of the most famous games to demonstrate this point was played by Paul Morphy (1837–1884). As you play through the moves, see how white appears to pull ahead in development, even sacrificing material in order to avoid having to break from his attack.

Paul Morphy – Duke of Brunswick (*Paris, 1858*)

1. e4   e5
2. ♘f3   d6
3. d4   ♗g4?

We have learnt from this game how bad this move is. Counter-attacking the centre with 3...♘f6 is better.

4. d×e5!

White forces black to exchange off his only developed piece, and at the same time speeds up his own mobilisation .....

4. ...   ♗×f3
5. ♕×f3   d×e5
6. ♗c4   ♘f6
7. ♕b3!

..... immediately gaining time by developing with the double threat of 8.♕×b7 and 8.♗×f7+. Black, in order to avoid losing material, is forced to block in his own Bishop.

7. ...   ♕e7
8. ♘c3   c6
9. ♗g5

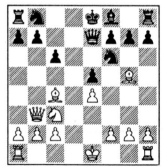

Fig. 72

White is ready to castle on either side!

9...   b5?

Black should be trying to unravel his pieces by 9...♕c7 and 10...♗e7. Now, instead of retreating the threatened Bishop, white sacrifices a Knight.

10.♘×b5!   c×b5
11.♗×b5+   ♘bd7
12.0–0–0   ♖d8

Black's King is caught in the centre. All his developed pieces are defending d7. His King's Bishop and King's Rook lie useless, unable to help. All white's pieces, on the other hand, are ready to spring into action wherever they are needed. It is little wonder then that white wraps up the game with a short, sharp finish.

13.♖×d7!   ♖×d7
14.♖d1   ♕e6
15.♗×d7+   ♘×d7
16.♕b8+!!   ♘×b8
17.♖d8 mate.

Openings

There are many different ways to open a game of chess; far too many to give here in any detail.

The following are the most popular, with brief descriptions of the main ideas behind them.

King's Gambit (1.e4 e5 2.f4)

This is a popular *gambit* (offer of material, usually a pawn). White plans, after 2...e×f4 3.♘f3 d6 4.♗c4 h6 5.d4, to dominate the centre, recapture the pawn and develop his

Fig. 73

attack along the open f-file. Black may decline the sacrifice by 2...♗c5 (when 3.f×e5?? loses to 3...♕h4+ 4.g3 ♕×e4+ and 5...♕×h1), or may counter-gambit by 2...d5.

Sicilian Defence (1.e4 c5)

The most popular reply to 1.e4. After an exchange of pawns in the centre, usually by 2.♘f3 d6 (or 2...♘c6) 3.d4 cxd4 4.♘xd4 ♘f6 5.♘c3, black tries to utilise the half-open c-file for his Rooks.

White plays for a kingside attack, placing his pieces so that they control the important strategical square d5 and trying to hit black's position with a timely e5.

Fig. 74

French Defence (1.e4 e6 2.d4 d5)

Very solid. Black aims to put a pawn in the centre at the cost of obstructing his Queen's Bishop.

This opening leads to slow, cramped positions for black with the long-term promise of an excellent middlegame.

White normally plays 3.♘c3, 3.♘d2 (hoping that black will surrender the centre by 3...dxe4), or the immediate 3.e5.

Fig. 75

Ruy Lopez (1.e4 e5 2.♘f3 ♘c6 3.♗b5)

One of the oldest and most respected openings, the Ruy Lopez, or *Spanish*, arises from sheer logic: both sides place a pawn in the centre and then try to defend their claims. Most of the theory concentrates on 3...a6 4.♗a4 ♘f6 5.0–0 ♗e7 6.♖e1 b5 7.♗b3 d6 supporting black's central pawn on e5.

Fig. 76

Queen's Gambit
(1.d4 d5 2.c4)

Not a true gambit, since white can always regain the pawn after 2...d × c4, yet with the same aims – undermine the centre. Black defends by 2...c6 or 2...e6

Fig. 77

King's Indian Defence
(1.d4 ♘ f6 2.c4 g6
3.♘c3 ♗ g7 4.e4 d6)

The KID is based on the theory that it is not necessary to fill the centre with pawns to control it. By means of the *fianchetto* of his Bishop to g7, black hopes to control the game from the flanks. Later black will choose between ...c5 and ...e5.

Fig. 78

The middlegame

So now you have developed your pieces to active squares and castled your King into safety. Now what?

The phase which follows the opening is known as the *middlegame*. This is the point where you should settle down and consider your battle plan – will you attack your opponent's King? Will you take over the centre and push your opponent's pieces back? Or perhaps you might pressure his queenside with your Bishops and try to pick up a few pawns?

The choice has to be made, and made with care. It is better to have a plan and stick to it than have no plan at all.

Who is better?

Look at the following positions and imagine that you have been asked to take the pieces and continue the game. How would you assess the positions and begin to choose a continuation? In each case, bear in mind the following aspects.

• *The tactical situation.*

31

- *The material situation.*
- *The position of the pieces.*
- *The pawn structure.*

In fig. 79, white is winning on material – he is a Bishop ahead! If the remaining pieces were to be exchanged he would be able to use that extra piece and his King to harass and capture black's pawns, and that would win easily!

Your immediate plan should be to actively exchange as many pieces as possible, without compromising your position or allowing black the chance to conjure up a counter attack. 1.♕×f6 exchanging Queens immediately is the wisest move.

Fig. 79

Marinelli – Manca
(*Italy, 1990*)

Fig. 80

In fig. 80 white is ahead on material – but this time by just a pawn. You would assume that black would avoid material exchanges, yet these constitute black's most powerful plan, since with each exchange white will find it harder to defend his material advantage. Indeed, after the forcing 27...♘c4! black goes on to win his pawn back and the game finishes quickly: 28.♘×c4 ♕×c4 29.♖b2 ♗×c3 30.♘×c3 ♖×b4 31.♖×b4 ♕×b4 32.♕d3 ♘e5 33.♕e3 ♕b2

34.f3 ♕c2 35.♔h2 ♘c4 36.♕d4 ♘d2 37.♔h3 ♕c1 38.♘e2 ♕h1+ 0–1

In fig. 81 below it is clear that material is level. Neither side appears to have a clear shot at a kingside attack.

Should white offer his opponent a draw – a chance to share the point?

Fig. 81

This is a good illustration of a situation in which you have to be able to identify certain *positional* features, so that you can set about choosing a logical plan to pursue into the middlegame.

Positional features

When we refer to *positional features*, we normally mean the arrangement of the pawns on the board. This is because wherever your pieces are placed, you always have the option to manoeuvre them to better squares. Pawns, however, tend to settle into patterns known as *pawn structures* which have distinctive characteristics and which influence the placing and value of your pieces. It has been said that 'pawns are the soul of chess...'

Common pawn structures

It is crucial to distinguish pawn structures, which are permanent and fixed, from *dynamic* pawn structures, which are temporary and transient features of the position.

Whilst the pawn is nominally the weakest and least valuable piece on the board, there are many situations, especially during the endgame, in which the pawn comes into its own. (As we have noted, the pawn is an especially dangerous tactical weapon precisely *because* it is the least valuable of all the pieces.)

In general, however, a pawn weakness will show itself more and more clearly as pieces are exchanged and there are fewer potential defenders.

Passed pawns

A pawn that can advance to the eighth rank and promotion without being blocked or captured by opposing pawns is said to be *passed*.

In the game (*see* fig. 82) **Timman–Agdestein** (*Mexico, 1985*), white began by creating a passed pawn in the heart of black's position by 23.♕d6! Black had no choice but to exchange Queens, since 23...♕e8 24.♗×e6 would have lost a pawn.

23...♕×d6 24.e×d6 ♘ec6 25.b5 ♘a7 26.b×a6 ♖c6 27.a×b7 ♘×b7 28.d7 ♖d6 29.♘e5 ♘c6 30.♖ab1 ♘cd8 31.♖fc1 ♔g8 32.♖c7 ♘a5 33.♖b8 ♘c4 (fig. 83) 34.♖×d8 ♖×d8 35.♖c8 ♖×d7 36.♗×e6+

Fig. 82

White wins material after 36...♔f8 37.♗×d7 1–0

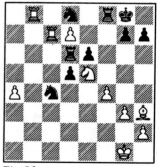

Fig. 83

Isolated pawns

An isolated pawn is one which stands alone, with no pawns of the same colour on the adjacent files.

Disadvantages

An isolated pawn cannot be defended by another pawn. Because of this, one or more pieces may become tied to the defence of an isolated pawn to prevent its capture.

Moreover, an enemy piece placed on the square in the path of the pawn blocks the advance of the pawn and cannot easily be shifted. In fig. 84, black's Knight occupies the excellent central square d5, in front of the isolated d4 pawn, from where it *blockades* the pawn and can play a part in the battle on both sides of the board. White cannot move the Knight.

In fig. 85, the only difference in the position is that white now has a pawn on c2. He can now play 1.c4! and the Knight must give way.

Advantages

An isolated pawn allows a piece to become established on either of the two squares which it controls (e5 and c5 in fig. 84). It also allows your

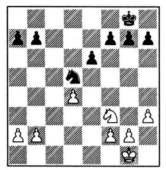

Fig. 84

Fig. 85

Rooks to become active on the two resulting open files, along which they can operate freely.

In the following example, white gives a perfect demonstration of how to play against the isolated pawn.

Flohr – Vidmar
(*Nottingham, 1936*)

Fig. 86

First, white begins by blockading the pawn with his Knight. 14.♘d4! ♖ac8 15.♕d2 a6 16.♗c2 ♕g5 17.f3 ♗d7 18.♖fe1 ♖fd8 19.♖ad1. He then adds pieces to the attack on d5 – ♕f6

34

20.♗b3 ♗a4 21.♗×a4 ♘×a4
22.♖c1 ♘c5 23.♖ed1 ♛b6 24.♘e2!
– intending to exchange Queens, after
which the weakness of black's pawn
will be highlighted. 24...♘d7 25.♛d4
♛×d4 26.♘×d4 ♘e5 27.b3 ♚f8
28.♚f1 ♖×c1 29.♖×c1 ♘c6
30.♘×c6 ♖c8 31.♖c5 b×c6

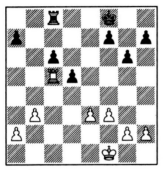

Fig. 87

Black's one isolated pawn has become
a set of *hanging pawns* (adjacent pawns
on open files), which – unless black
can contrive to advance them by...c5 –
will become very weak. White has a
blockade set up and immediately
brings his King into action, to the

commanding square d4. 32.♚e2 ♚e7
33.♚d3 ♚d6 34.♖a5 ♖a8 35.♚d4
f5 36.b4 ♖b8 37.a3 ♖a8 38.e4 f×e4
39.f×e4 d×e4 40.♚×e4 ♖a7 41.♚f4
h6 42.h4 ♚e6 43.♚g4 ♖a8 44.h5
g5 45.g3 ♖a7 46.♚f3 ♖a8 47.♚e4
♖a7 48.♚d4 ♚d6 49.♚e4 ♚e6
50.♖e5+ ♚d6 51.♖e8 c5 52.♖d8+
♚c6 53.♖c8+ ♚b6 54.♖×c5 Finally
the c-pawn is lost. 54...♖h7 55.♖e5
♚c6 56.♖e6+ ♚b5 57.♚f5 ♖f7+
58.♖f6 1–0

Anchoring your Knights: outposts

Because its sphere of influence does
not extend very far, the Knight is best
placed in a central position. The Rook,
Bishop and Queen can attack the
central squares and the enemy
position from afar. The Knight,
however, can reach otherwise
inaccessible squares and, placed
securely, can create havoc.

In the following position, white
finds a powerful pawn sacrifice which
gives his Knights excellent outposts on
c5 and e4 to add to the one he already
commands at e6.

Lasker – Capablanca
(St. Petersburg, 1914)

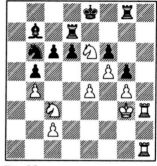

Fig. 88

35.e5! d×e5 36.♘e4 Threatening a
Knight fork by 37.♘×f6+ 36...♘d5
37.♘6c5 ♗c8, black is forced to give
up the exchange in an attempt to hold
his position 38.♘×d7 ♗×d7 39.♖h7
♖f8 40.♖a1 ♚d8 41.♖a8+ ♗c8
42.♘c5 1–0

Doubled pawns

Two pawns sitting on the same file are
said to be *doubled*. Doubled pawns can
be very weak, since they impede each

other's advance and may easily be blockaded. In fig. 89 you can see that black's kingside, crippled by doubled pawns, easily falls under the combined assault of the white pieces.

Polgar – Yudasin *(Germany, 1991)*

26.♕×f6! White is not afraid of black's passed pawn. 26...c3 27.♘e4 c2 28.♕h6 Intending 29.♘f6+ ♚h8 30.♕×h7 mate 28...♝g6 29.♘f6+ ♚h8 30.♘e8! With the unstoppable threats of either 31.♕f8 mate or 31.♕g7 mate 1–0

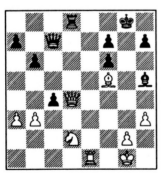

Fig. 89

Backward pawns

A *backward* pawn is one which can no longer be supported by adjacent pawns.

The difference between an isolated pawn and a backward pawn is that whilst an isolated pawn *cannot ever* be defended by another pawn, a backward pawn has been temporarily left behind by pawn advances on adjacent files.

Fischer – Petrosian
(Buenos Aires, 1971)

Fig. 90

In this position white has broken up black's pawn formation with ♝×♘c6,

in the process saddling black with an isolated pawn on a6.

Black, it seems, can easily advance his backward pawn by...c5 – but he never gets the chance, since white has too much pressure on d5. 11.0–0 c5? 12.d×c5 ♝×c5 13.♝×f6 and 14.♘×d5.

White plays to open the c-file against the weak pawns. 11.0–0 0–0 12.♖fe1 h6 13.♝h4 ♕d7 14.♖e2 a5 15.♖ae1 ♝d8 16.b3! ♖b8 17.♘a4! ♘e4 18.♝×d8 ♖b×d8 19.♕f4 ♕d6 20.♕×d6 c×d6 21.c4 ♘f6 22.♖c1 Making ready to occupy the open c-file – 22...♖b8 23.c×d5 c×d5

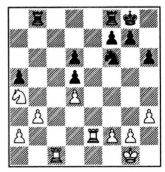

Fig. 91

36

White went on to win the endgame, capturing all three of black's isolated pawns in the process!

Pawn chains

Pawns often become locked together in *chains*. The exact arrangement of the pawns in a chain can be determined as early as the first three or four moves, depending on the choice of opening variation.

This can dictate the course of play, as both players attempt to break up the chain and gain more open lines for

attack and freedom of movement for their pieces.

A pawn chain can be besieged at the *head* or the *base* of the chain.

In fig. 92 white will play for f4–f5. Black will either play c7–c5 or f7–f6 and try to exchange his *bad Bishop* for white's *good Bishop* by... ♗a6.

Note A Bishop whose movement is restricted by its own pawns is said to be a *bad* Bishop. Likewise, a Bishop which can move freely is termed a *good* Bishop.

In fig. 93 white will play for c4–c5. Black will either play f7–f5 or c7–c6.

Rooks need open files!

When a few pawns have been exchanged, open files become available for the Rooks to operate on. From c1 the white Rook attacks every square on the c-file. The black Rook controls the *half-open* f-file.

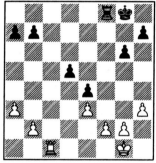

Fig. 94

French chain

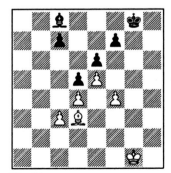

Fig. 92

King's Indian chain

Fig. 93

Seventh and eighth ranks

If a Rook can reach the seventh or eighth ranks unchallenged, its power increases tenfold. This is because it hits not only the squares along the file but also the pieces and pawns still on the ranks to the left and right of it.

In **Reti – Colle** (*Baden–Baden*, 1925 – *see* fig. 95) white tried to connect his Rooks with 1.♔d2? ♘f3+! This fork forced white to capture, leaving the seventh rank clear for black's Rook. 2.e×f3 ♖h2+ 3.♔c1 ♕e2 4.♕d8+ ♔h7 0–1

Keres – Petrosian
(*Bled*, 1959 – *see* fig. 96)

The weakness of the eighth rank led to a brilliant finish after 1...♕×f4+! (deflection) 2.♕×f4 ♖h1 mate (back rank mate).

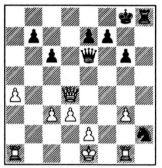

Fig. 95

Fig. 96

Attacking the castled King

As with mating attacks, there are also thematic ways to smash your opponent's King position. The sacrifices illustrated below should provide some inspiration.

×h7 motifs

Greco's Sacrifice, stemming from an analysis published in 1619:

1.e4	e6
2.d4	♘f6
3.♗d3	♘c6
4.♘f3	♗e7
5.h4	0–0
6.e5	♘d5

Fig. 97

7.♗×h7+! ♔×h7

Black could refuse the sacrifice, but would remain a pawn down.

8.♘g5+   ♔g8

8...♔g6 9.h5+ ♔h6 10.♘×f7++ ♔h7 11.♘×d8 wins the Queen.
8...♗×g5 9.h×g5+ ♔g6 10.♕h5+ ♔f5 11.♕h3+ ♔g6 12.♕h7 mate.

9.♕h5	♗×g5
10.h×g5	f5
11.g6 wins	

×g7 motifs

Timman – Hubner
(Tilburg, Netherlands, 1988)

Fig. 98

22.♘×g7! White aims to drag the black King out to where he can be mated.

22...♔×g7 23.♕g5+ ♔h8 24.♕f6+ ♔g8 25.♕g5+ ♔h8 26.♕f6+ ♔g8 27.♖b3! White threatens an instant win with 27.♖g3+ and mate 27...♖e8 28.♖g3+ ♔f8 29.♖g7 ♖e7 30.e6 ♗×e6 31.♖×h7 Since he cannot even safely avoid 32.♖h8

mate (black would have to play 31...♔e8 32.♖h8+ ♔d7 33.♖×a8 with mate to follow), black resigned. 1–0

×h6 motifs

M Gurevich – Yudasin *(USSR, 1984)*

Fig. 99

18.♗×h6! Black's pieces are not in a position to repel a sacrificial attack. 18...g×h6 19.♕d2 White plans to play ♕×h6 and ♕h7/8 mate 19...f6 20.♕×h6 ♕g7 21.♕×g7+ ♔×g7 22.♖h7+ ♔g8 23.♖×b7 ♘a5 24.♖×a7 ♖×c3 25.♗b5 ♘b3 26.♖d7 ♖fc8 27.g3 1–0

×f7 motifs

Chigorin – Steinitz
(Havana, Wch., 1892)

Fig. 100

19.♘×f7! ♚×f7 20.e6+! White's sacrifices draw the black King into the centre like a magnet. 20...♚×e6 21.♘e5 ♛c8 22.♖e1 ♚f6 23.♛h5 g6 24.♗×e7+ ♚×e7 25.♘×g6+ ♚f6 26.♘×h8 ♗×d4 27.♖b3 ♛d7 28.♖f3 28...♖×h8 29.g4 ♖g8 30.♛h6+ ♖g6 31.♖×f5+ 1–0

Attacking the queenside

Just as a pawn move in front of the King can give you a concrete target to attack, so in many cases does moving a pawn, by c3 or...c6, to support your centre.

The minority attack

The minority attack is a good illustration of the above and arises quite often in the *Queen's Gambit* (*see* below).

The difference is that white attacks the black queenside, which consists of *three* solid pawns with his own *two* queenside pawns, and hopes thereby to leave black – after exchanges – with a terminally weak pawn on a half-open file.

Queen's Gambit
Nikolic – Ljubojevic
(Amsterdam, 1988)
1.d4 ♘f6 2.c4 e6 3.♘f3 d5 4.♘c3 ♘bd7 5.c×d5 e×d5 This is the basic position in which white must choose either to attack the black King

(perhaps castling queenside, with a sharp game); or, by the minority attack, ensure a steady if slight advantage in the middlegame. 6.♗g5 ♗e7 7.e3 0–0 8.♗c2 c6 9.♗d3 ♖e8 10.0–0 ♘f8 11.h3 ♘g6 12.♗×f6 ♗×f6 13.b4! a6 14.a4 ♗e7 15.b5

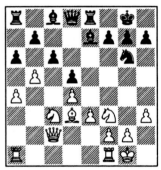

Fig. 101

15...a×b5 16.a×b5 ♗d7 17.b×c6 b×c6 18.♘a4! White has achieved his first aim and now makes plans to occupy the outpost with his Knights. 18...♖a5 19.♘d2! Bringing the other Knight to the queenside 19...♛c7 20.♘b3 ♖a7 21.♘ac5 ♗c8

22.♖×a7 ♕×a7 23.♖a1 ♕c7
24.♘a6 ♕b6 25.♘bc5 ♗d6 26.♖b1
♕a7 27.♘b4 At last the c-pawn is
won. Note that 27...♗×c5 28.♘×c6!
♕c7 29.♕×c5 wins the pawn safely,
whereas 27...♗×c5 28.♕×c5?? ♕×c5
29.d×c5 blocks white's half-open file,
exchanges off his excellent Knight and
gives him his own pawn weakness, the
isolated pawn on c5, to worry about.

Fig. 102

27...♕e7 28.♘×c6 ♕g5 29.♔h1
♘h4 30.♖g1 ♕f5 31.♘e5 f6 32.♘f3
♕h5 33.♖e1 ♘g3+ 34.f×g3 ♗×g3
35.♖f1 ♖×e3 36.♘e4 d×e4
37.♕×c8+ ♔f7 38.♕b7+ 1–0

Planning for the endgame

When you have learnt more about the
various endgames, you will find that
in the middlegame – even in the
opening – it is possible to think ahead
to the endgame and judge whether
you could win the resulting position.

Put at its simplest, if your opponent
loses a pawn early on and you are
confident playing pawn endgames,
then you should aim to exchange as
many pieces as possible.

This not only prevents your
opponent from generating a counter-
attack as compensation for his
material deficit, but simultaneously
increases the *real* value of your
material advantage. You should also
ensure that your King is ready to be
brought into the centre of the action
should an endgame arise.

Good and bad pieces

In fig. 103 black has a *bad Bishop*,
hemmed in by its own pawns. White
has a *good Bishop*, which can move
freely about the board and, in an
endgame, can harass the black pawns
which are fixed on dark squares.

However, in this game white
exchanged off his good Bishop. Why?

Sher – Mestel (*Hastings, 1990*)

Fig. 103

23.♘b2 h5 24.h3 h×g4 25.h×g4
♘h4+ 26.♔h1 ♔f7 27.♗e1 ♖h8
28.♗×h4! ♖×h4+ White is in no

danger from the black Rooks, since he can challenge and exchange them off along the open h-file. The important feature of the position – the factor which will give white a decisive advantage – is that white has (by 28.♗×h4!) exchanged off black's only decent piece. This allows the white Knight to dominate the game completely from the c4 square (and later the c6 square). His Knight also prevents the black Queen from penetrating the white position. 29.♔g2 ♖ah8 30.♖h1 ♕a7 31.♘c4 ♔e7 32.♖×h4 ♖×h4 White manoeuvres to challenge the black Rook. 33.♖f1! ♕a8 34.♕e1! ♗f6 35.♖h1 ♕a7 36.♕a1 ♕d4 37.♕×d4 e×d4 38.♖d1 ♖h8 39.♘×a5 ♔d7 40.♘c6 From c6 the Knight supports white's passed pawn which threatens to promote by a4-a5-a6-a7-a8, prevents black's Rook from taking the open c-file, and attacks both black's weak pawns on b4 and d4. Black must inevitably lose material.

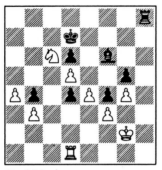

Fig. 104

40...♖c8 41.♖h1 (Not the impatient 41.♘×b4? ♖b8 42.♘c6 ♖×b3 or 41.♘×d4? ♗×d4 42.♖×d4 ♖c2+ 43.♔h3 ♖c3 unneccessarily complicating the game.) 41...♔c7 ♔c7 42.♔f2 d3 Black gives the pawn up in order to give his Bishop the diagonal 43.♖d1 ♗c3 44.♖×d3 ♔b6 45.♖d1 ♖h8 46.♔g2 ♔c5 1–0

The endgame

What is an endgame?

The endgame is the final phase of the game, usually occurring after the Queens have been exchanged and neither player is likely to be able to mate by a direct attack on the opponent's King.

Basic endgame principles

The following principles hold true in most endgames.
- **Activate your King**– by bringing it towards the centre.
- **Create weaknesses in your opponent's pawn structure** that may be infiltrated by your pieces and later by your King.

- **Improve the position of your pieces and exchange your bad pieces**. Likewise exchange your opponent's good pieces and leave him with a bad Bishop, a Knight stuck out on the edge of the board.
- **Do not hurry!** Endgames require patience. Sometimes you may have to spend time attacking one side of the board to create a weakness, and then gain the winning advantage on the *other* side many moves later. Rushing to attack a weak point may actually throw away your winning chances.
- **Exchange pieces when ahead on material**. Always be aware of opportunities to transpose into a won pawn endgame.
- **Consider pawn moves very carefully** – pawns are the only pieces that cannot move backwards, so a mistaken pawn move cannot be easily rectified!
- **Passed pawns must be pushed** either to promote them or to tie your opponent's pieces down by using the *threat* of promotion.
- **Be aware of the stalemate trap and other drawing ideas**, with either side.

King and pawn endings

All endings boil down to King and pawn endgames in the end.

It is important to remember that just one extra pawn is enough to win the game – if you know how to win the endgame.

The opposition

The *opposition* is a kind of zugzwang which occurs very frequently in pawn endings. Study fig. 105. In this, the simplest of endings, white can win by forcing the black King to retreat using the opposition.

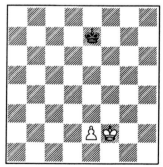

Fig. 105

1.♔e3! ♔e6 2.♔e4 (gaining the opposition) 2...♔d6 3.♔f5! ♔e7 4.♔e5 (again black is forced to give way) 4...♔f7 5.♔d6 ♔e8 6.e4 ♔d8 7.e5 ♔e8 8.♔e6! ♔f8 9.♔d7! White wins absolute control over the queening square of the pawn 9...♔f7 10.e6+ ♔f8 11.e7+ ♔f7 12.e8♕+ and wins. Note that white only draws by 1.e4? ♔e6 2.♔f3 ♔e5 3.♔e3 ♔e6! 4.♔f4 ♔f6! This time it is black who gains the opposition. 5.e5+ ♔e6 6.♔e4 ♔e7! 7.♔f5 ♔f7 8.e6+ ♔e7 9.♔e5 ♔e8 10.♔f6 ♔f8 11.e7+ ♔e8 12.♔e6 stalemate.

The square

When defending against a single pawn you can draw if you can get close enough to stop the pawn from queening – i.e. if your King can get into the *square* of the pawn.
In fig. 106 on the next page, white to move wins easily with 1.h4 ♔c6 2.h5 ♔d6 3.h6 ♔e6 4.h7 ♔f6 5.h8♕. Black to move steps inside the square of the pawn and easily captures the pawn with 1...♔c6! 2.h4 ♔d6 3.h5 ♔e6 4.h6 ♔f6 5.h7 ♔g7.

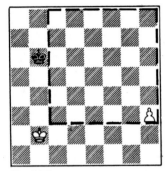

Fig. 106

Counting moves

In fig. 107 black gets the opportunity to exchange off all the pieces into a King and pawn ending. Assessing the position as winning for black is a matter of simply counting moves. This is a useful method to apply in pawn endgames where visualising the position on the board might prove difficult!

Vaganian – Lautier
(Manila, Philippines, 1990)

Fig. 107

44...♗a4 45.d4 ♕×d4! 46.♕×d4+ c×d4 47.♔b2 ♗×b3 48.♔×b3 ♔g6

Fig. 108

Black sees that it will take white *nine* moves to capture the d-pawns and promote his c-pawn by ♔c2-d3×d4-d5×d6 and then c4-c5-c6-c7-c8♕. Black, however, only needs *eight* moves to promote by ♔h5-g4×f3-e3 and f5-f4-f3-f2-f1♕. Therefore he will promote first. This enables him to visualise the resulting position. 49.♔c2 ♔h5 50.♔d3 ♔g4 51.♔×d4 ♔×f4 52.♔d5 ♔e3 53.♔×d6 f4 54.c5

44

Fig. 109

54...f3 55.c6 f2 56.c7 f1=♛ 57.c8=♛ ♛f6+! 0-1 Whatever white's reply, black can force the exchange of Queens with a simple win in the resulting King and pawn ending, e.g. 58.♚d7 ♛f5+ or 58.♚c7 ♛c3+.

Rook and pawn endings

Rook and pawn endgames are more common than any other. This is because the Rooks are normally the last pieces to be brought into action and, consequently, the last to be exchanged.

It is frequently said that 'all Rook and pawn endings are drawn'. This is because the Rook is such a powerful and agile piece that materially balanced Rook endgames require a delicate hand to win

Korchnoi – Timman
(Hilversum, Netherlands, 1982)
In the endgame, a passed pawn becomes both a lethal threat to promote and a useful decoy to tie down enemy pieces.

In Rook and pawn endgames both the defender and the aggressor must try to get their Rook *behind* the passed pawn where it wields the most power.

In fig. 110 white formulated a winning plan which consisted of:
• exchanging the Queens
• pushing the b-pawn to the seventh rank to tie the black Rook to b8
• advancing the white King to attack the black pawns
• using the Rook to attack the black kingside from the *flank*, until it is possible to win more material or create a passed pawn (probably the h-pawn)
• advancing the passed pawn to promotion.

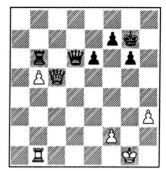

Fig. 110

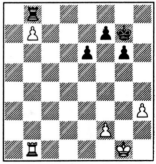

Fig. 111

[1.] 33.♕×d6 ♖×d6 [2.] 34.b6! ♖d8
35.b7 ♖b8 (See fig. 111.)

36.♔g2 ♔f6 37.♔g3 ♔e5 38.♔g4
[3.] f6 39.h4 ♔d6 40.♖b6+ [4.] ♔e5
41.f3 ♔d5 42.f4 e5 43.f5! Not
actually *gaining* material, but
artificially creating a passed h-pawn.
43...g×f5+ 44.♔×f5 ♔d4 45.h5 e4
46.♔f4 ♔d3 47.h6 e3 48.♖b3+
♔d2 49.♖×e3 ♖×b7 50.♖h3 [5]
Nothing can prevent white from
promoting his pawn. 1–0

Minor piece endings

Knight against Knight
Knights are particularly vulnerable to
passed pawns, especially *outside* passed
pawns (on the flanks), since the
Knight cannot cover ground fast
enough to catch them. (*See* fig. 112.)

M Gurevich – Dolmatov *(Germany)*

50.♔f2 ♔f6 51.h4! d5 If 51...♔e5
then 52.h5! ♔×d4 53.h6 and the
pawn Queens. 52.g4 c5 53.g5+ ♔e5

Fig. 112

Fig. 113

54.h5 1–0

Knight against Bishop
In general, *blocked positions* and
positions with pawns on one side of
the board will tend to favour Knights,
whereas *open positions* with pawns on
both sides of the board should favour
the player with the Bishop.

In fig. 114, white's Knight is clearly
better positioned than the black
Bishop. It can travel to all the
important squares without restriction,
whereas the 'good' Bishop is trapped
by the phalanx of white pawns and is
unable to come to the defence of the
crippled kingside. Because of this,
white is able to forcibly exchange off
the black Bishop by ♘f3-e5 and
decisively penetrate the queenside
with his King.

M Gurevich – Anand *(Italy, 1992)*

45...♔e8 46.♔c3 ♔d7 47.♘f3 ♔e8
White has the constant threat of ♘h4,
which ties the black King down.
48.♔c2! ♔f7 49.♘e5+! ♗×e5
(Otherwise white wins a pawn with
50.♘×g6) 50.f×e5 ♔e7 51.b3!
Opening up a path for the monarch.

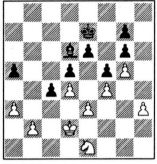

Fig. 114

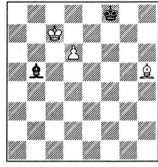

Fig. 115

Fig. 116

51...♔d7 52.b×c4 d×c4 53.♔c3 ♔c6 54.♔×c4 a4 55.h4 1–0 White has the opposition, and wins after either 55...♔b6 56. d5! e×d5+ 57.♔×d5 ♔c7 58.♔e6! ♔d8 59.♔f7 when the e-pawn Queens, or 55...♔d7 56.♔b5.

Bishop endings
Endgames featuring Bishops of the same colour are common. If there are fixed pawns, then the side with the better Bishop will have the winning chances.

In fig. 115 the immediate attempt to Queen the pawn only draws, since

1.d7? ♗×d7! leaves white with insufficient force to checkmate. White only wins because he is able to drive the black Bishop away from the diagonal by 1.♗f3! intending 1...♗a4 2.♗c6 ♗×c6 3.♔×c6 ♔e8 4.♔c7 winning, or 1...♗e8 2.♗c6 ♗h5 3.d7.

Bishops of opposite colours
Endings with Bishops of opposite colours are often drawn due to the inability of either side to challenge or exchange off the opposing Bishop.

In fig. 116 black cannot win despite being two pawns ahead, since white can hold the b-pawn with his King on b3, and if black attempts to win by 1.♔b3 ♔d4 then simply 2.♗f5 draws.

However, it is also true that the combined forces of a King and a Bishop cannot be met with equal resistance. Therefore you should attempt to fix your opponent's pawns on the same colour squares as your Bishop, where they may prove vulnerable.

Index